Little Rhymes For Life's Tough Times

Cora Dawson-Shaw

With love
Cora x

Copyright © 2022
All rights reserved.

ISBN: 9798371769671

with love,
Cora ♀

DEDICATION

I would like to dedicate this collection of poems to

My mum Hayley
And Grandparents Garry & Corinna
For helping me to become the woman I am

My Husband George
For helping me love the woman I am

My Counsellor Diane
For helping me understand the woman I am

CONTENTS

1	Introduction	Pg 10
2	Introjected Values	Pg 16
3	The Therapist	Pg 17
4	Anxiety	Pg 18
5	Nest	Pg 19
6	Panic Attack	Pg 20
7	Dancing	Pg 22
8	Palpitations	Pg 23
9	Paper and Pen	Pg 24
10	Instinct	Pg 25
11	Music	Pg 26
12	Friends	Pg 27
13	Self-Worth	Pg 28
14	Coffee	Pg 29
15	I am not	Pg 30
16	I am	Pg 31
17	What you see	Pg 32

17	What I see	Pg 33
18	Wishes	Pg 34
19	Amygdala	Pg 35
20	Vitamins	Pg 36
21	Toxic Friendship	Pg 37
22	Numb	Pg 38
23	Ouch!	Pg 39
24	The Holidays	Pg 40
25	Perfect Version of you	Pg 42
26	It's okay to be selfish	Pg 43
27	Selfish	Pg 44
28	Family	Pg 46
29	Hard Days	Pg 47
30	Dark Days	Pg 48
31	Sunshine	Pg 50
32	The Secret	Pg 50
33	100 Versions of you	Pg 51
34	My Family	Pg 52

BOOK TITLE

Introduction

I would like to start this book off by saying thank you for buying it, reading it or even just picking it up, if it's in your hands it means my dreams are coming true!

My name is Cora and at the time of writing this book I am 30 years old; I have dreamed for as long as I can remember of being a wealthy and successful woman with a mark to leave on the world but have never been sure of how or what. That is until recently when all the pieces of my past experiences started to fall into place creating this idea for me to write something I could share with you.

I have struggled greatly with my mental health for most of my life, but things took a real turn for the worst at the age of 19 when I became pregnant and the change in hormones had the most catastrophic effect on my mental health ultimately resulting in my decision to terminate the pregnancy and seek medical help.

I mainly struggle with health anxiety, but this also carries over into some general anxiety too and ultimately an unhealthy fear of mortality, this in turn has led me into some very dark periods of depression and unhealthy relationships both with people and things such as alcohol, shopping, promiscuity and food, although not all at the same time.

I think it's important for me to say here that I have not been an 'alcoholic' in the recognized sense but the relationship I had with alcohol was unhealthy all the same. For me the problem was that I spent so much of my day to day feeling anxious and up tight constantly risk assessing my surroundings and my health with what ifs that when I had a few drinks all that worry and tension would just melt away, to some that might sound relaxing but to me it was the start of becoming an "unstoppable moron" as I like to call it. Once the shackles of anxiety were off, I would behave promiscuously with little care, I would drink far more than I could handle and there were times I acted against the law with a careless attitude. All the things I would never do sober, and I would go on to regret this until the next time. Mostly this was only a weekend habit but there were periods where it became more. An example of this is one Christmas period where I spent most days over a 10-day period intoxicated, sadly this did result in me being sexually assaulted, something I have only recently come to terms with. These experiences along with many others though have brough me to where I am now… 7 years sober, very clear on what I want to achieve and living a full, happy and loving life.

The shopping is a beast I am still trying to tame but an ongoing problem for a very long time, I recognize this is like most things a short-term buzz at the detriment to the long-term outcomes, so I try to have periods of not buying anything.

Like most people enjoy feeling comfortable, happy and healthy in my body and for me that sits around a size 12 but rather than enjoying that long term goal I have often gone for the short-term happiness of unhealthy eating and drinking habits that have led me to somewhat yoyo between a size 8 (unhealthy for me) and a size 16 (unhappy for me) I have been working mostly on this recently and seem to be doing okay, but we are not perfect and I'll fuck up on something else, but that's okay I'm at peace with that because I have the knowledge and the will power to turn it back around.

I recognize I have been incredibly fortunate to have had supportive friends and family around me to help me survive the toughest times and enjoy the not as tough times but regretfully I have also seen a lot of friends come and go with the difficulties mental health issues can bring to a friendship.

My reason for sharing these intimate parts of my life with you is in the hope that you can feel my sincerity and emotion in my writing, and I only hope that if you relate to anything at all I've written that it shares a message of acceptance and belonging. We all have history we've all had our share of shit at some point, and I feel you!

In the last 10 years I have worked incredibly hard on helping myself survive with the mental health I have got; this has included various methods of therapy both private and not, of which all have served some purpose and groundwork for me to build on, but I must be honest and say there has been no magic cure for me in this realm. I have done extensive reading and learning in numerous methods and theory around mental health improvement and why we think the way we do and how life experiences from the past can affect how we act and feel in the future both consciously and sub consciously. This is something I have taken a deep interest in along with the immersive world of positive thinking and mindset importance which I hope will be illustrated in my creative writing.

With my growing passion for self-improvement and the realization that I am certainly not alone with these issues I started to reach out to others with mental health struggles, partially because it helped me to feel more normal and less like an alien but also because I wanted to share my knowledge and helpful tips with people who might find it useful in their own survival. This led me to set up a mental and emotional support group for women in my local area MESS Mental and Emotional Support Sisterhood, this was an incredibly proud achievement, I couldn't believe people turned up to something I had organized and especially around such a delicate subject. But they did and the group grew to two and saw around 50 different women attend before covid came along and stopped me in my tracks. This realization though that people were interested in how I might be able to help them and the stark reality that we were all struggling to get support from a medical perspective until crisis point or face a waiting list stretching months and months is what has driven me to look harder at helping others to feel less isolated and alone in what they're experiencing.

My hope for this book is to make people suffering feel less alone and able to relate to someone else struggling with their mental health, also maybe help somebody understand better a loved one who struggles. There are hundreds of books and media online full of helpful information, but I want this to be a slightly playful way of looking at a serious subject and hopefully in turn making it more accessible and more relatable.

Introjected Values

On the day that I was born my family gave to me
A gift I did not ask for a way for me to see

It was a pair of glasses for me to see the world
The glasses they were tinted not sparkly or pearled

I wore the glasses blindly through school and growing up.
Till one day I started thinking, what the actual fuck

These glasses are no good for me they distort what I believe
The tint that's been put on them is stopping me achieve

I took off those damn glasses and saw through my own eyes
Such hope and positivity brough a welcoming surprise

All this time a dissolution that life is hard and tough
But now I see it differently and I can't get enough

Opportunity there is plenty and money to go round
They said it was impossible to have a million pound

Achievable now I see it though others jeer and scoff
It's time for me to live my life and take those glasses off!

The Therapist

A Truth you see like no one else
Unfiltered and stripped my real self.
My pain reflected upon your face
In the words you say with empathetic grace.
I know in here you will not judge
For my past and opinions, you'll hold no grudge.
I feel safe with you to share and let go
Of my anger, my resentment, my sorrows and woe.

But also, we laugh, and you make me feel proud
That I've learnt so much and I can say out loud,

That I'm worthy
I'm great
A good person
A great mate
I'm caring
I'm funny
I'm cleaver
And wise
And I deserve to be happy
Without using disguise.

So, thank you so much to my therapist indeed
For every situation you're the person that I need.

Anxiety

I feel you within me there bubbling away
Just waiting for a trigger to come and ruin my day.

The pit in my stomach and the lump in my throat
Leaves me quivering and hiding behind the hood of my coat.

I know that you're with me I can sense that you're here
Because everything I see through a darkened lens of fear.

I battle against you with logic, and I fight you with doubt
But it's so hard to hear myself unless I really shout.

Then people think I'm crazy!!!

Nest

It is where I feel comfy, safe and warm

It's a hot sunny day laid out on my lawn

It's in the arms of my husband

My bed and a film

Hot bubble baths

Or laughter with friends

Its fields in springtime

The smell of fresh coffee

Its freshly washed bedding

Cuddling the dog or my teddy

My Nest is where I'm comfy, safe and warm

Panic Attack

That dreaded awful moment, you feel it take a hold
Your skin and face are flush, but your blood feels to run cold.

Your palms they just start sweating, you need a toilet quick
Your vision's going blurry, feels like you might be sick.

There's a lack of concentration, and focus has gone too
It's hard to hear and understand what anyone says to you.

Your heart starts beating faster, but you're talking feels slow
You try to carry on with life, but the worry starts to grow.

A churning in your stomach and a lump inside your throat,
It's difficult to swallow so it's time to get your coat.

Your instinct is to leg it, but your logic says sit tight
You know this panic will go again and then you'll feel alright.

You close your eyes and count now, deep rounds of breath
Even though it feels like it, you know this is not death.

So go on little panic attack, you are not needed here
I was fine before you came along and there's nothing for me to fear.

Dancing

A vision I am dancing

With one hand in the air

Laughing open mouth

Like nobody will care.

I worry over nothing

Feel free and full of fun

As I dance and sing out loudly

Beneath the summer sun.

A vision I look happy

Both outside and in

As I greet the planets people

With my genuine happy grin.

I don't care their opinion

For it matters to me not

Whilst I am out here dancing

Shaking everything I've got.

Palpitations

With every flipping flutter

My fear fills me more

Forgetting how to function

Just focused on the floor

Just fuck off palpitations

You're not welcome anymore

That flipping fluttering feeling

That shakes me to my core!

Paper and Pen

I've found no greater magic than in paper and in pen
I sometimes need reminding though every now and then.

Writing on a page, what's trapped inside my head
Helps me slow my racing mind before I go to bed.

Scribbling a letter to pass on to a friend
Explaining how they've hurt me, although I'll never send.

Jotting down ideas of things, I'd like to do
It helps me plan my future with a clear and positive view.

Penning out a Hinch list or things I need to buy
So, I don't need to remember although I like to try.

Drawing out a picture of a dog or a wedding dress
I'm certainly no DaVinci but it helps to ease my stress.

Noting down my goals, helps me to set my mind
So, I can achieve the life I want, and leave settling behind.

The greatest films and music come from paper and from pen
They make so much achievable for all us women and men.

Instinct

When we were all just cave men,
Our instincts must be strong
But now its twenty something
I feel I'm wired wrong

There is not sabertoothed tiger
Prowling at my door
So why when I hear a knock
Does my sweat start to pour?

My heart will race
And adrenaline rush
When I walk in the dark
At the rustle of a bush.

Just one wrong word
That I might overhear
Leaves me curled in a ball
Consumed by fear.

A dash for the exit
As my mind choses flight
When all I want
Is to go out for the night.

Worst I can't sleep
Coz my brain thinks there's danger
But I'm so bloody tired
I could sleep in a manger.

Music

Sometimes I like classical music

Some days I prefer rock

I like Johan Back

And massive attack

My mood changes round the clock

I like music soft in the background

I also enjoy it up loud

Depends on my mood

If I'm being subdued

Or if I'm raving away in a crowd

I sometimes use music to uplift me

But it also calms me down

It's great in the morning

If I'm still yawning

I can dance in my dressing gown

Friends

Friends are all so different

It's good to know between

The ones who've got your back

And the ones that can be mean.

Some will be supportive

Some will just know best

Some will be your bridesmaids

And others will be a guest

Self-worth

I know that I am worthy

Of affection, love and time

I do not need to seek it out

The most important love is mine.

I give myself what I deserve

And you should do that too

Because if anyone deserves your time

It is definitely you.

Coffee

The thing about coffee is this

Sure, I know that it tastes good

Wakes me up

With just a cup

Then makes my bladder flood

But the fun just doesn't end there

Three beats for the price of one

My heart races

Beats in the spaces

Plus, it makes me eat cakes and bun

So, my herbal tea doesn't look as cool

Can't Instagram my Starbucks cup

But keep your bean

And your caffeine

Coz its chamomile I choose to sup

I am not

I am not anxiety

I am not depression

I am a fighter

This is a lesson

I am not taboo

I am not a secret

I am on a journey

You would not believe it

I am not disorder

I am not unable

I am living proof

Getting betters not a fable

I am

I am compassion

I am strong

I will not give in

This far along

I am a success

I am driven

I take all the chance

I have been given

I am improvement

I am perseverance

I'll achieve greatness

Without interference

What you see

A shining smile

Telling of jokes

Revealing clothes

No need to coax

Centre of attention

Acting a clown

Dancing around

No sign of a frown

Singing along

Posing for pics

Flicking my hair

Shaking my hips

Causing some mischief

Twerking my bum

Oozing out confidence

Having some fun

What I see

Put on a front

No one will know

It's hard getting ready

I'm feeling so low

Laugh very loudly

So, people can't see

That really, I'm crippled

With my misery

Keep moving my feet

And dancing all night

So, they cannot see

I'm riddled with fright

I make out a wish

That I'm home in bed

But I'm here pretending

To be okay instead

Wishes

Make a wish they tell you

But don't tell anyone

For if you say it loudly

The magic will be gone.

Why should we keep our wishes

Locked up in the dark?

Where they are much less likely

To set off with a spark.

Let's make our wishes known

And share what's in our souls.

They're more likely to be granted

When our wishes look like goals.

Share your wishes proudly,

Don't keep them all hush hush.

Sometimes all they need to feel

Is a tiny little push.

Amygdala

This little part of brain, responds very quick

It's the part that makes us panic; it can be a little prick.

It's there to help survival, so we can fight or run

But my amygdala's broken, it ruins all the fun.

A photo of a spider, is no danger here to me

But this little bit of brain thinks it's time for me to flee.

It sends out the adrenaline and cortisol too

Making me all sweaty and running to the loo.

Vitamins

We are what we eat

And I think it's good to know

The foods that are unhealthy

And the ones that help us grow.

But did you know that also

Some effect our mental health

And when it comes to self-care

I think that knowledge is wealth.

Magnesium and omega 3

Are good for our mind

In fish and in dark chocolate

These vitamins you'll find

Nuts and avocado

Are good to try too

But also eat bananas

If you like to eat your fruit

Toxic Friendship

I should cry… but I wont

I could sigh… but I don't

I walk away with my head held high

And reflect on the time that's passed us by.

I think of you everyday

I think of things I could say

But I keep to myself these things I feel

And I hope that in time these wounds can heal.

I don't know where did it start?

That our friendship was falling apart

In the blink of an eye this change had come

And suddenly our time had run out of fun

I still hold a place in my heart

If ever there can be a restart

For you will always be special to me

From this toxic friendship though I must be free

Numb

Music is playing

Bodies are swaying

Chatter of tongues

Singing of songs

I take it all in

Clutching my gin

But I'm in a trance

No desire to dance

People of plenty

But I feel empty

Got nothing to say

Just reply "I'm okay"

My body is here

But my spirits not near

I feel hollow and shell

Like I'm under a spell

I should just go home

But then I'm alone

And I don't know what I might do!

Ouch!

So, I put myself right out there
I didn't want to, but I tried
The outcome wasn't brilliant
It hurt me and I cried

My confidence and ego
completely blown to bits
and when I think I've forgotten about it
the reality comes back and hits

I fought against my instinct
to stay in my comfort zone
And now my only wish is
that I would have stayed at home

My soul feels bruised and battered
My heart sad and blue
Next time I'll stick to my comfort place
And leave the excitement to you

The Holidays

I think I should be happy now

And spreading Christmas cheer

What would people think of me

For hating this time of year

I can't stand all the food around

And people getting pissed

Even though I'm 30 though

I still write out a list

I wish for peace and happiness

No toys or games for me

I'd just like to enjoy myself

And maybe feel free

I see photographs of parties

Perfect family greetings

For me it is not like that

Mine is work and AA meetings

I try and do my best though

Pretend I'm in the mood

Ill have a glass of orange juice

And gaze at all the food

If I'm to be honest though

I'll be glad when this is done

My memories over Christmas time

Have not always been much fun

Perfect version of you

There isn't that much to be certain of

But this one I know to be true.

Out of everyone you meet in this world of ours

There is only one version of you!

It doesn't matter what size you are

What you wear or whatever you do.

So perfectly perfect at being yourself

There's no way there could ever be two.

It's okay to be selfish

when your little they say don't be selfish

we are taught that its bad and not right,

but you know what is worse than being selfish

leaving yourself as an oversight.

It's okay to do what YOU want to

No need to feel guilty or mean.

Because if all that you are is selfless

It's not great for your own self esteem.

Selfish

When people say I'm selfish I take it in my stride
For they don't know I really see what they have implied

The one who deems me selfish has not got their own way
Their tactic is to guilt trip me into doing what they say

But me I see right through it I know where the truth lies
Your selfish claim is empty, and I see through its disguise

I call it looking after me and pleasing just myself
For no one else can do it well It's for my mental health

I like to please others too but sometimes it's too much
For who will do what I want when I need that extra touch

So, you can call me selfish when it doesn't go your way
But actually, I do not care, not yesterday or today

I am the most important, my hands hold my own health
And friends who cannot see this don't let me be myself

It's not bad to be selfish or do just what you please
It's you that makes your happiness so life can be a breeze

Family

The funny thing about family is

You can't really pick and choose,

And no matter whoever's child you are

You don't need to follow their shoes.

Some say that family is everything

And others say anything but.

So, no matter who your family are

It's okay to trust your own gut.

Hard Days

Some days are harder than others

Some days are harder still,

But some days get much brighter

And some days you will feel brill.

It is harder to remember

That good days always follow,

When your swaddled up in blankets

Of doom, gloom and sorrow

Dark Days

Some days are darker than others
Some days are darker still
The fact that I'm still here though
Without a potion, scar or pill

It shows a strength I'm proud of
It isn't something everyone's got
It's the thing that keeps me pushing on
When I could end it all and rot

It's not one I feel often
But I've had some scary days
When I've considered ways to end my life
Though tears, fog and haze

But I will not go out like this
And I'll tell you gladly why
I know what my brain is telling me
Is nothing more than just a lie

Some days they can be dark
But I've had these days before
I know that round the corner
There are happier days for sure

It breaks my heart to read the words
Another life is lost
Because I know I could have helped them
If only our paths had crossed

I know that bitter feeling
Like there is no other way
But I also know that down the line
These feelings will not stay

I hope that if you're out there
Feeling lost and dark
You know I feel it with you too
And those days have left their mark

But we can keep on going
I can promise this
Because no life is bad enough
To throw into the obis

Dark days there are plenty
But lighter days are more
And know that if you're reading this
You're in my heart for sure

Sunshine

The sunshine makes me happier

I hear it and feel it too

But why do I put all my eggs in its basket

Like the sun makes my wishes come true.

It's time to take the power back

Embrace the cold and dark

The sun only makes things brighter

But the glow comes from my heart.

The secret

There is a little secret

Not everybody knows

The more you think about it

The more and more it grows.

It doesn't matter good or bad

If you want it or if you don't

But if you think about it long enough

Eventually it shows.

100 versions of you

Did you know there are hundreds of versions of you?
Not like clones or robots though like R2-D2

But versions that people who meet you see
In the shops or at school or when you're out for your tea

It's a difficult concept to understand really
But I like to imagine all my versions walking freely

To some you are free maybe joyful and happy
Yet to others you'll always be knee high in a nappy

Online you might be confident, rich or sarcastic
To some you could come across as hollow and plastic

But it's something that I find fun and worth knowing
Because the best thing is that every version keeps growing

My Family

Nobody is perfect you've got to admit
And often enough someone acts like a tit

But I know in my soul just how lucky I am
To be a certified member of our Shaw clan

I know I am loved and held so dear
Respected and cherished every day of the year

For that I am thankful and so much more
In sickness and health for richer or poor

Your guidance and teaching throughout generation
Has laid for me this exciting foundation

With freedom to explore and find for myself
My passions, my dreams and personal wealth

For me there is no family better than mine
With love and support to last my lifetime

My mum gave me morals and empathy no end
Showed me how to love and be a good friend

My grandmother gave me the passion to write
And the vocabulary knowledge to rhyme it alright

My Grandfather shared with me his musical flare
And a way to debate if I ever should dare

Thanks to you my family tree
Without all of you I wouldn't be me

Printed in Great Britain
by Amazon